MICHELLE FEAGIN

Blessings always,

Michelle

Breadcrumbs

A PSALM 46:10 JOURNEY

Clear Wind
PUBLISHING

Breadcrumbs: A Psalm 46:10 Journey

Clear Wind Publishing

Library of Congress Cataloging-in-Publication Data is available.
ISBN: 9798218090760

Table of Contents

For Charlie

We will always remember all the love and laughter
you shared so freely with us.

Coming home from work each night with treats in your shirt pocket for the boys; sitting in your chair and letting them climb all over you to get them; making sure each one got his share of candy and hugs. Getting baptized first so the boys would know it didn't hurt. Taking Matthew to the doctor for his shots when I had to work and returning home devastated because he cried. Sitting on the floor playing blocks with the boys and sharing their joy when they knocked over each tower. Taking an hour to get home from work in an ice storm because you had to stop by my mother's home first to make sure she had everything she needed. Being my right arm and anchor at every attorney meeting and court date. Laughing hysterically while trying to stuff a two-year-old into a down-filled jacket. Spending countless hours finding books on Native American culture for the boys.

Being everything a Daddy and a husband should be.

Foreword

I t is a rare honor to write the foreword for a book. The author is asking you to introduce them and provide some context for the book.

So it is my honor to introduce this book and its author. By way of preview, I am a child and adolescent psychiatrist with a long history of working with, and learning from, children and families impacted by various forms of developmental adversity and trauma. The nature of this clinical work is such that children and families come into your world at a time of crisis, you do your best to help, and then, mostly, the child or family moves on. Sometimes physically, sometimes emotionally—no longer requiring the same level of support. In some very rare and special situations, you may have the opportunity to learn how these struggling children and families are doing. This is one of those rare and special moments for me.

Over 20 years ago I met Michelle and her children. She was a foster parent who had opened her home and her heart to three young boys. Their mother was a member of a Native American (First Nations) tribe in the United States. She had struggled as a parent and the children had been removed from her care by child protective services (CPS). As you will read, the process of bringing the three brothers together and into Michelle's home was complicated. Each of these boys had some strengths and some struggles—as you would expect following their challenging start in early life. Michelle brought these boys into her home, and ultimately to our clinic.

Our clinical team started to get to know the unique developmental journeys of these boys—we wanted to know what had happened to them so we could better understand and help them. A centrally important part of their history was their connection to the people of this First Nations community. As we are beginning to better understand, connections to family, community and culture are the bedrock of health in all domains: physical, social, emotional, and spiritual. This book is an illustration of this.

But what happens when connection to family and culture are not in synchrony? What happens when an attentive, attuned, responsive and loving person brings children from a different culture, race, or ethnicity into their home? The safe, stable, and consistent love in this home is a positive, but how can the racial and cultural ties (that are also important throughout life) be provided? All too often, in our racially and culturally diverse society, this situation results in conflict, as you will see in this book. Rarely does the conflict help the children. Our society tends to set up an antagonistic situation between the foster or adoptive parent and the child's culture of origin.

The beauty of this book is the description of the relentless, hopeful love that helped reconcile these conflicts; the process of re-connecting the boys to their culture and First Nations community is an example of how respect, compassion and goodness can overcome our society's tendency to set up "blame and shame" solutions to complex challenges. Parenting is difficult; in today's society it is even more difficult; foster parenting and adoption add more challenges; doing so across race and culture compounds and magnifies all of this. But love is powerful—the love of a parent for these boys and the love of a people for the future of their tribe—and when both combine, selflessly, the results are amazing.

Bruce D. Perry, MD, PhD

Preface

I must confess to being a flip flopper. I don't actually see that as a bad thing. It just means I give myself the right to think about things once in a while and be open to a new point of view. One of my favorite sayings **used** to be: *A coincidence is a minor miracle where God has chosen to remain anonymous.* That one's way overdue for the recycle bin!

Does God *really* choose to be anonymous? Or could it be that we are just too overwhelmed by all the daily noise to hear Him? Can we not see the breadcrumbs He casts down to us each day because we are too busy looking for the big picture? Who can notice a string of breadcrumbs in all of that and still follow the trail? **Be still and know that I am God** (Psalm 46:10).

My favorite sermon of all time was on that short, wonderful verse. My pastor read it and said that everyone reads it wrong. Then he exclaimed, **"BE STILL!"**

Long   silent   pause

"Know that I am God." Hearing it that way knocked us off our pews. This was a whole new way of comprehending that message. I have signs throughout my home now with this statement because I need a lot of reminding.

Breadcrumbs

During our four-year struggle to adopt our three boys, our string of breadcrumbs made the manna in the desert look like an ant hill. Each person placed in our path led to the next one, ready to run their leg of the race. Just a few of them included:

- 7 attorneys

- 5 judges

- a radio station employee

- a radio talk show host

- a juvenile justice volunteer

- a newspaper reporter

- multiple TV news anchors

- child psychiatrists with special connections

- an adoptive Mom with the tribal council ...

Well, you get the idea. Unfortunately, most of these wonderful people have moved on with their careers, and we have lost touch. But they are forever in our hearts. Come to think of it, getting laid off from my dream job in Illinois and having to start over at the bottom of the ladder in Texas was a big part of making this all possible. Funny how devastating things can turn out to be blessings in hindsight. These are just a few of my breadcrumbs. I share them with you gladly in hopes they will help you spot yours—and see Who is sending them.

Chapter One
AFGHANS AND ANGELS

T hey say life begins at 40. *They* weren't kidding! Several years ago, I was in a whirlwind of fear over the welfare of my great-nephews. They were living in terrible conditions and my attempts to intervene had been fruitless. None of the social services seemed concerned about these three little guys. They were four years, two years, and three months old, and hardly able to fend for themselves. All I could do was fret, pray, and turn 40.

On a miserably cold March day, I was completely unable to focus on my work. I left the office hoping an escape for lunch would clear my head. Just one problem; I had no appetite. Perhaps browsing through the nearby resale shop would clear my head. It was worth a try. Rummaging about the shop, I spotted a beautiful baby afghan at the irresistible bargain price of $1.00. It had obviously been hand-made with great love. I picked it up thinking how nice it would be to give this to the baby.

Just as quickly, I threw it back on the shelf. How stupid! I'll never get a chance to see the baby or even get this to him. Forget it! I moved along the aisle trying to re-focus. Something grabbed me by the collar and pulled me back to the afghan. I picked it up again. It was so soft and inviting. How could it be priced at just a dollar? Again, I threw it back down, a bit more irritated with myself. This is ridiculous! There must be something in this shop to catch my attention. Maybe they have something I can use in the kitchen.

Once more I felt my collar being snatched and pulled back down the aisle. Once more I found myself rubbing the afghan. Was there a magnet on that spot on the floor? Finally, I snatched the stupid afghan and marched over to the cashier, throwing it down on the counter. Words can't express how irritated I was with myself for doing something so pointless. I headed out to the parking lot and threw the proof of my early senility into the trunk and returned to work.

When I arrived, one of my coworkers rushed frantically toward me. She told me CPS had been trying to reach me for the last half hour and thrust a pink phone message into my hand. I raced to return the call and was told the baby had been abandoned. They needed me to come and pick him up to care for him until they could find the mother and work things out. I don't know what the speed limit was, but I'm sure I broke it racing over there.

A circle of ladies was cooing at a little one. "Is that Matthew," I asked. They smiled at me and nodded, making room in the circle. It was love at first sight when I saw Matthew. Somehow, through it all, he managed to give me a huge smile. I was hooked. All he had for clothing was an undershirt and a diaper. It was freezing outside. But I just *happened* to have a cuddly warm baby afghan with me! I wrapped him up and snuggled him in my arms. I've never seen a baby look so peaceful. Perhaps the angel that kept grabbing my collar was still with the afghan, singing lullabies to him.

It didn't matter that I had no idea where to start, that I had nothing but the afghan to use to care for him. Or that I had no idea how to reunite him with his brothers. Somehow, I knew I would be directed through it all, just as I had been from the start in that resale shop—I would follow the rest of the breadcrumbs.

Chapter Two
HE'S ABOUT THIS LONG

There's little to compare with the free-for-all caused by the sudden addition of a three-month-old child into an adult household. Instant is fine for coffee, but not so much with a baby! Steven Spielberg could have been directing the action.

The list was already zapping about through my rattled brain cells: diapers (quickly), powder, formula (what kind?), baby food (is he ready for that yet?), baby shampoo, baby soap (do they make that?), baby towels, baby wash tub, clothes (how do they size those?), blankets (we have to wash the afghan sometime), baby detergent, baby bottles, pacifiers, teething rings (when does that start?).

I called my husband and mother and announced our new arrival. They were ecstatic. My mother rushed over like she had filled her car with rocket fuel. After ooh's, aah's, and tears, we started to put a plan together. Food needed to take priority. We had no idea when he had been fed last. Since this area needed the most expertise, I stayed at home with him while experienced Grandma took grocery store duty. She returned with everything to fix a proper feast for a baby. He seemed quite satisfied, so she must have gotten it right. She also guessed well on diapers, which were definitely needed by now. Of course, she had Mom and Grandma skills, and I was clearly out of her league.

My turn. With my credit card firmly in hand, I raced to the mall. Much to my dismay, I discovered that buying baby clothes requires some crucial data. Size 15–30 pounds? Length 24–36 inches? Oh great! A clerk eventually came over to see if she could help. My description was around three months old, and about this long, and feels like about 20 pounds—maybe.

SECURITY!!!

It's a miracle she didn't think I had abducted this child. Fortunately, she took pity on me and helped me select items with our best deductive reasoning. Sherlock Holmes had nothing on us that day.

Once again, some master planner seemed to know when all this was going to happen and made sure someone helpful would be in my path. I left the store confident I would not look like a total amateur when I returned home. My mother sorted through the items and gave me her approving nod and smile. My mood switched from confusion and insecurity to rewarding accomplishment.

We were finally able to clothe Matthew with something more than a diaper and an afghan. With a full tummy and two women cuddling him, I doubt he much cared about such details. He did look quite cozy in his new duds, as he drifted off to a very secure sleep. Somehow, we had gotten through the first hurdle. We turned the couch around in the guest bedroom, so it faced the wall. Voilà–– instant crib! It would do until we could deal with that. Of course, that would be taken care of for us too. We just didn't know it yet.

Charlie broke a record getting home. "Where's the baby?!" he cried. He couldn't wait to see him for the first time and was equally smitten when he did. Walking past all the bags and receipts, he never asked a word about the new expenses. None of that mattered to him. He was totally on board. Soon a crib arrived from the daughter of my manager at work. A friend brought a changing table and dresser. My mother curled some ribbon and hung strands above the crib and changing table. We had a real nursery! It almost looked like I knew what I was doing. I was totally on top of this, as long as God left plenty of angels busy on the case.

Chapter Three
ORDER IN THE COURT

O nce the turmoil settled down and we were able to begin some new kind of normal, it was time to try to find Matthew's brothers and bring them all back together again. Of course, we had no idea where to start. It turned out that my work associate had a client who was an attorney working in family law. Wasn't that a helpful *coincidence*? Oh right, I don't use that word anymore.

I called and explained the situation, and he set a time for us to meet. He was unavailable but had another attorney in his office who had just finished her case and was able to help us immediately. She filed the necessary paperwork to obtain a hearing for us. Within a short time, we were ready to attend our first court date. Little did we know this was just the first of many over the next four years— yes, four! We had two objectives that day. The first was to obtain official custody of Matthew with the blessing of CPS. The second was to get temporary custody of his brothers, Mark, and Michael. They had been placed in foster care and it would take a court order to reunite the boys.

By now, Matthew had really gotten the hang of eating. He filled up every chance he got. This resulted in multiple diaper changes as we awaited our turn before the judge. Each time I left and entered the courtroom, the judge seemed to scowl a bit more. It was obvious he had many years on the bench and had little patience left for disruptions. Matthew, of course, was oblivious to all of this. Just when there was a lull in the activity and the room was quiet, he let out a contented belch that sounded like a tornado alarm. The judge's scowl reached to the bottom of his chin. There were lines on his face that even his staff had not seen before. The bailiff darted over to us and told us we needed to keep the baby quiet. Obviously he was not a father. Only someone who never had children would think meeting such a demand was possible. Finally, our case was called, and we sheepishly went up before the judge. He looked like he would rather sentence us to six months than grant our petition.

Our attorney went into great legal detail presenting our request, while he sat there looking in dire need of an aspirin. When she finished, he asked where the birth parents were. She explained that the father was in jail and the mother refused to go into rehab to honor the foster care agreement she signed for Mark and Michael. She had left Matthew with a neighbor and never returned. Her location was unknown. His disposition changed completely. He gave us a warm smile and reviewed the papers on his desk. He looked up and asked if we were willing to take in all three children. What was completely natural to us seemed to be an incredulous idea to him. Our response was an overwhelming *yes*.

Then he looked at our attorney. "The parents are doing drugs?" I don't have an adjective for how angry he looked.

"Yes, judge."

"Permanent custody of Matthew is awarded to Charles and Michelle Jenkins! It is also ordered that temporary custody of Mark and Michael be awarded to Charles and Michelle Jenkins. Those children are to be made available to them within 24 hours."

This grandpa didn't have any use for parents who abused drugs or alcohol. Then he smiled at us and motioned us to come closer. With a Santa style wink, he gave us one admonishment. "Promise me one thing. As loud as he is, please don't let him grow up to be a lawyer!"

We chuckled and offered our pledge. We left the courtroom the thrilled instant parents of three boys. Taking on three kids aged three months, two, and four just might be a bit challenging for newbies, but we could only think about all the hugs we would be sharing. I like to think we brought a bit of sunshine into the work of that judge that day. Hopefully, it made all the difficult times seem worthwhile. We were certainly glad he was our judge. How did we ever get assigned to the docket of that crotchety grandpa? Something to ponder.

Chapter Four

REUNITED AND IT FEELS SO GOOD

The next day I got a phone call from the foster care agency. Mark and Michael would be in their office by 3:00 PM. (It seemed like it would never be 3:00!) The boys had stayed with us twice when the family was homeless, so they knew us. The question was, would they remember us? We hadn't been able to see them for several months, and so much had happened to them during that time. How would they react to coming home with me? Would I seem like a stranger?

Mark was two and very shy. He stood hiding behind Michael, trying to be invisible. Michael was four and was struggling to be the big brother, giving him some semblance of assurance. Both boys seemed to vaguely remember me, but they were full of anxiety.

We signed the paperwork quickly, and I tried to reassure the boys. They were very quiet as they left the building and got in my car. After we had gone a few blocks, Michael looked at me and just asked, "Matthew?" It was then I realized they had no idea what had become of their baby brother. How upsetting that must have been for them! I told him Matthew was at the house and they would see him in just a few minutes. It seemed to be difficult for him to comprehend. All the way home he kept asking, "Matthew?" I kept trying to reassure him, knowing that only seeing his brother would make things okay again for him.

When I opened the front door, Matthew was in the living room, cuddled in Grandma's lap. Michael ran through the door and jumped over both of them. He kept crying, "Matthew!" It seemed like he would never let go. Mark worked his way into the pile and all three boys were embroiled in one giant hug, with Grandma somewhere in the mix. It looked like a football huddle on the five-yard line.

After a while, the boys began to relax. Memories of staying with us seemed to be coming back. Michael pointed to the TV and asked, "Puppies?" It took me a minute to get that one. Then I remembered the video we had of *101 Dalmatians*. They had watched that movie non-stop when they were with us before and loved it. I quickly grabbed the movie and showed it to him. Both boys grinned and started feeling at home again.

I put the movie in the VCR and hit the play button. They settled on the carpet in front of the TV and looked content for the first time in a very long while. This time I had a little bit of notice to do some prep, so I had cups with lids and straws ready and waiting. I brought them into the living room, filled with apple juice and accompanied by a bowl of cheese curls. Life was good!

On the TV, Pongo was looking out the apartment window, little knowing how much his life was about to change. The same could be said for the boys. That seemed a bit ironic to me. I don't know if they would have made the connection with us as quickly without that movie. I was very glad I had bought it for them the last time they stayed with us. Fortunately, I had been guided to make that purchase at the time. How amazing that a simple movie would become a tool to ease two traumatized little boys through the transition to their new life with us. It's like someone knew it would be needed.

Chapter Five
THE CHRISTMAS VILLAGE SCENE

I n some ways it does take a village to raise a child. It certainly was the case with three instant kids! CPS and the court had basically handed us three little boys with the clothes on their backs and wished us a nice day. We didn't get nine months to get ready. It was hit the starting blocks and sprint!

As word spread among our friends and coworkers, loving bundles began arriving at work and at our home. Bags and boxes filled with gently used clothes and toys just kept coming. If anyone asked what clothing sizes we needed, the response was that it didn't matter. Everything would fit someone sometime. It was almost like a Dr. Seuss book. There were diapers and t-shirts and blue jeans and socks, pull toys and bouncy balls and boxes of blocks. We arranged the clothing on the shelves by size with lots of boxes marked for growing-into sizes. The toys were scattered randomly all over the house. That was going to be a constant for several years.

Our first Christmas was even more overwhelming. By then, half of Houston heard of our three little waifs. We wore a path in the carpet answering the front door. Storing everything out of sight was quite a task. Fortunately, the kids were too little to spend time in the garage, so that was our North Pole Central. We lost track, but I'm sure it was at least 2:00 on Christmas morning when we finished wrapping everything. It took a while to find the dog under all the scraps of paper and bows. Thank goodness he snored. Then came putting everything under the tree. Our living room shrunk significantly.

The bounty was so plentiful that it was a two-man job to plug in the tree. An experienced parent would have done that first. Charlie held onto my left arm while I dangled helplessly over the mountain of gifts to reach the outlet. It would have made a great trust building exercise for any corporate retreat. When the boys stumbled out of bed and came into the living room, they just stared blankly at the scene. They had no idea what to make of it. They certainly had never experienced a Christmas like this!

It was amazing how everything turned out to be exactly what was needed, although none of our Christmas elves had coordinated this avalanche of love. It was as if some master planner had worked it all out. And we hadn't even made a list!

Chapter Six

THE GREAT WALL

I should probably take a time-out here to clarify the dynamics. Our going joke when trying to explain it to people is that we don't have a family tree. We have a family bush! It's reminiscent of the country western song with the lyrics, "I'm my own Grandpa." Here goes.

My late sister would have been the boys' grandmother. Her son, Terry, was the birth father of the two youngest, Mark and Matthew. Michael's father was unknown. So technically, I was their great-aunt, and my mother was their great-grandmother. My sister had passed away long before they were born, so it fell to me to jump in.

So technically Michael wasn't related to us. They all shared the same birth mother and that was all that mattered to us. We didn't believe in half-brothers. No one was a half person in our house. Matthew simplified it when he learned to talk. "We were *borned* together, so we have to stay together." Can't really improve on that.

Their birth mother, Yvette, was a full blooded Apache. My nephew, Terry, was blond with freckles. Mark had his features and Matthew had hers. Michael's father must have been either Hispanic or African American. He had much darker features than his brothers. He was surprisingly aware of it for such a young child.

The other movie we had saved for them was *The Jungle Book*. They loved that one too. One day I noticed Michael looking at his arm when Mowgli was in the scene. He was making comparisons. It obviously bothered him and made him feel like the odd man out. If that weren't enough, he and Mark had been shuffled through multiple foster homes over the few months before coming to live with us. Trust was a very tall order for him.

We found a highly recommended child psychiatrist and took him to visit with her. After a few sessions, she told me she was completely unable to get through to him. She said she had never seen a child with such an incredible wall built up. But she did offer some hope. She referred us to Dr. Bruce. He was gaining a national reputation as being at the top of his field in working with children who had experienced trauma. She felt if anyone could get through the wall, it would be him.

With her introduction, we were able to meet with him. Getting in the door would never have happened without her help. The waiting list for new patients was endless. Once he learned the situation, he asked that all three boys come together for sessions with him and his staff. They needed to see their interaction and it would also help lower Michael's defenses if he wasn't singled out. The sessions continued for several years as he chipped away, brick by brick.

There were lots of interesting activities in the waiting room. The boys loved playing with the large wooden train track that swirled in every possible direction. I enjoyed watching them while awaiting our sessions. It was always a challenge for the receptionist. Michael's last name was Johnson, Mark and Matthew's last name was White, and my last name was Jenkins. When I was engrossed in watching the boys play, I often didn't pick up on the first attempt or two.

"Mrs. White?"

"Mrs. Johnson?"

Oh, they want me. "Here we are."

It really didn't matter to me which name they used. I quickly got used to answering to any of the three options.

Occasionally my mother would pick them up from daycare and take them to their session if my work schedule ran late. She played a big part in their care and reassurance. Grandma hugs are great therapy. On one of the times I was taking them, the traffic was worse than usual. Houston traffic is bad on a good day—impossible on a bad one. They tended to get upset when things weren't on schedule. I glanced toward the back seat and told them not to worry. It would be okay if we were a little late. Mark popped up to reassure me.

"It's okay, Mommy. You can make it. Just drive like Grandma!" She didn't appreciate the humor when it was relayed to her later. That happens when you're totally busted by a three-year-old.

After a few months, we noticed the boys' behavior was changing. They had been very shy and quiet. They stayed in their room a lot or huddled together watching TV. Then suddenly they seemed to have their heads spin around like the scene in The Exorcist. They became completely different kids, rambunctious and scattered in every direction. I was sure I must be doing something terribly wrong to have caused this reaction.

I talked to Dr. Bruce on our next visit about this complete reversal. I was bewildered, to say the least. He looked like he was very glad to hear the update. That confused me even more. He leaned forward grinning and said, "I have good news and bad news. They're getting comfortable." They were starting to feel secure enough to test the boundaries now. That was good to know, but it also meant we were in for some new challenges. Our parenting just got kicked up a notch! We felt very blessed to be in the caring and brilliant hands of Dr. Bruce. Little did we know the history he had that would be even more invaluable down the road. But more about that later.

Chapter Seven
NOW YOU SEE IT ...

A s we moved from challenge to challenge, doubts inevitably crept in. Were we doing what we wanted, or was this God's call to us? It was difficult to be sure sometimes. I felt like Moses needing to tap that rock a second time. I recently had the privilege of attending the annual luncheon for the Mission of Yahweh, a wonderful oasis for women and children escaping crisis situations. Their guest speaker was David A. R. White. I sure wish I had heard him talk back then!

If you're not familiar with him, he started Pure Flix productions, developing films for Christian audiences when it was unheard of. He told his story about going from working in the Kansas wheat fields as a teenager to moving to Los Angeles at age 19 with a burning mission in his heart. Of course, everyone scoffed and thought he was crazy. Today, he has produced over 20 Christian films enjoyed by major audiences.

His presentation was the answer to my dilemma. Maybe it will be a shortcut for yours. At the time I was struggling to finish writing this book. The same question was buzzing in my mind once again. He addressed the question of how to know if something you wanted to do was God's will. He immediately had my full attention.

He said it boiled down to three simple things:

1. Is the idea bigger than you are?

2. Does it refuse to stop banging around in your head—**LOUDLY**?

3. Will it honor and glorify God?

He expanded on each point, but that's the gist of it. Sure wish I had been smart enough to figure that out way back then! But the timing was perfect to give me the confidence to finish this book. Funny how that *happened*.

Anyway, it was time for my annual checkup, which included a trip to my gynecologist. He looked concerned after completing the exam. He told me in as calm a voice as possible that I had a tumor and he needed to do a biopsy right away. I'm not sure any announcement had ever instilled that much fear in me. I managed to maintain a reasonable amount of composure until I reached my car. Then I burst into tears. I wasn't afraid for myself. I could only wonder what would happen to the boys if I wasn't here to raise them? I cried out, "Lord, you asked me to do this job. I need my health to do it. If raising the boys is your will, I need you to heal me so I can do it."

Somehow, I maneuvered through the traffic with misty eyes and put on a brave face for everyone when I got home. I decided to keep the news to myself until I had the test results. When I went for the follow-up visit, the doctor was scratching his head.

"I don't understand it. The biopsy results were clear. When I examined you again, there was no tumor! I know it was there. I clearly felt it during your last exam. But it's not there now!" He left the room, muttering to himself down the hallway. Back to the car. Time to finish the conversation.

"Okay, God. I get it. Now I know this is what you are asking us to do. No more doubts."

Chapter Eight
FINDING THE RIGHT DAY CARE

Matthew was very slow to start talking. The drugs and alcohol during his gestation took a toll. We knew we had to find a day care that would focus on speech and help him catch up. One of my coworkers had young children, and I asked him if he had any suggestions. He lit up and told me all about his son's day care. The lady who owned it had been a speech therapist in the school district. She put a big emphasis on helping the children develop verbal speech. His son also had speech delays and had made great progress there. Nice that we *happened* to work together.

I quickly checked out the day care and found it to be the perfect environment for him. Matthew loved the day care and felt at ease right away. He turned out to be quite the social butterfly and made friends quickly. I knew we had been led to the right place but didn't realize the full extent of it.

When we arrived one morning, a little boy was standing in the corner crying. Nothing seemed to help him. This was obviously not just an attempt for attention. He was clearly very upset. I asked the teacher what was wrong and was told it was his first week. He was having a difficult time adjusting. I picked him up and held him for a while until the tears stopped flowing. Then I put him down and tried to interest him in some of the toys. No dice.

He needed a buddy. I asked Matthew to give him a hug to make him "all better." Matthew looked at him with the serious concentration of a two-year-old trying to make sense of his world. Then he walked over to him and very gently picked up his hand. Looking into the boy's eyes, he softly kissed the back of his little hand, reassuring him. Then he led him off to investigate a big yellow truck. Mission accomplished. Clearly, there was another reason we were led to this day care. Someone else had some breadcrumbs of their own in play here.

I don't know if Matthew noticed that the child was black. If he did, it clearly made no more impression on him than the color of shoes he was wearing. Probably much less. All he saw was another little boy, who was upset. He wanted to help. Why is it so much easier to learn prejudice than to learn to make it "all better"? No wonder Jesus took such joy in the little children!

Chapter Nine

THE GAUNTLET

W e were starting to meld as a family. There would be challenges along the way, but for the most part, it should be smooth sailing from now on. We had permanent custody of Matthew and temporary custody of Mark and Michael. Our next court date was set to move their status to permanent custody. Then we could file for adoption.

Or not.

CPS had instructed us that visitation with the birth parents must take place in their offices for everyone's protection. They wanted to avoid any "he said/she said" problems, not to mention Amber alerts.

Yvette came to the house, along with two very large men we didn't know. Charlie and I were at work and my mother was watching the boys. She nervously raised the window and told her as calmly as possible that she needed to call CPS and set up a visit. We would be glad to bring the boys and let them spend time together. That did not go over well. They sped off in a car blaring hard rock music, and that was the last time we heard from her.

My mother called me at work, and I could hear the panic in her voice. I assured her she had done the right thing. I called our CPS caseworker so she would know what happened. She told me not to be concerned, but I could hear tension in her voice too. A few weeks went by, and we thought everything had blown over. Turns out the wind was much stronger than we realized, and the storm was blowing in our direction.

The doorbell rang, and I found a gentleman at our front door holding a large white envelope. After confirming my identity, he handed it to me with an apology. I'm no lawyer, but I could see it was a lawsuit filed over the kids. My heart sank. Apparently, Yvette had contacted her tribe and told them we were taking her children away from her. No doubt a few details were omitted. The tribe was taking us to court to move the case to their jurisdiction. We felt confident things would work out okay if the case stayed here. Our CPS caseworker and the judge both wanted to see the boys stay with us. But if the case was moved to tribal court? Game over.

We had never been blessed with children. The answer had remained—no. As a result, we had room to take in three kids. We felt God had delayed His answer to our prayers in order to reserve us for their need. What would happen if the tribe took over? How many families would be able to take in all three boys and keep them together? And how much more traumatized would they be with that change, just when they were finally learning to trust and feel secure?

Fear was beating out faith. I was a wreck. My stomach had more knots than a Boy Scout camp. It was all I could do to get through each day. My job was in sales. I drove around Houston each day on appointments. It seemed like everywhere I went there was a car in front of me with a KSBJ radio station bumper sticker saying, "**God Listens.**" I felt like rear ending the next one! God certainly hadn't been listening to *me* when I was crying and praying on my pillow every night.

One of those stupid bumper stickers finally got the best of me. I shoved my fist up toward the roof of the car and yelled, "I've got something for you to listen to!" I suddenly felt an incredibly warm hug embracing me and heard a softly whispered, "I know." Then I realized all those crazy people with those annoying bumper stickers were scattering more breadcrumbs for me. They led me from fear to faith. Ever since then, I've been another one of those crazy people driving around Houston with a "**God Listens**" bumper sticker. I hope and pray I can annoy someone else in need.

Chapter Ten
TWO STEPS BACK

O ur attorney told us frankly that our new complications made this case beyond her comfort zone. She recommended an attorney with more experience in family law cases. We met with Barry, and he advised us that a response needed to be filed in court within a few days. He would move this to top priority.

A short time later we were advised of our next court date. Charlie and I arrived with our nerves completely jumbled but anticipating a strong presentation for our case of staying in the Harris County court. We never made it into the courtroom.

The two opposing attorneys had been summoned into the judge's chambers to discuss the matter. Barry came out and talked with us in the hallway. Matthew's permanent custody agreement had been nullified. All three boys now had temporary custody status with us. Our hearts sank. The case would also be moved to a different court to be argued on the issue of jurisdiction rather than custody. It would be a full roll of the dice. Win, we stay a family. Lose … couldn't even think about that.

We decided not to tell the boys about any of it. They were too young to understand, and we didn't want to frighten them. It was better to let them keep adjusting to their new family life. Barry did his best to assure us that we were in capable hands. I'm sure he genuinely believed that, but he had never taken on a Native American tribe in court before. This was new ground for all of us. And very shaky legal ground.

The tribe's attorney worked solely as a litigator for Native American tribes. He was used to working in all levels of courts and it didn't faze him. His confidence could not be ignored. There was nothing we could do but pray and solicit prayers from everyone we knew. Our prayer team grew by leaps and bounds. Surely God had further plans.

Chapter Eleven
LET'S SAY A FEW WORDS

T here was nothing to do but press forward with the day to day needs of the boys. We had to use the AA prayer as our mantra.

Lord, give me the courage to change the things I can,

Accept the things I can't,

And the wisdom to know the difference.

Michael was ready to start Pre-K. He still spoke very few words. When he did, he was difficult to understand. He definitely needed speech therapy. With a big chunk of our budget going to the legal battle, there was no money for that. The school district did provide speech therapy for students and Michael would be able to receive that if we moved him from day care to Pre-K. There was one problem. Due to budget constraints, Pre-K was reserved for children who couldn't speak English. With a large Hispanic population in Houston, that certainly made sense. But we needed an exception to the rule.

I contacted the school district to try to get Michael enrolled. Each attempt fell on deaf ears. I kept being told it was only for non-English-speaking children. Frustrated, I bellowed, "The kid can't talk—in any language! He needs some help!" Nada. Then God told me to go in person and talk with the principal of our zoned school. I had little hope for this working out but grew tired of the same message playing in my head every night. So, off I went to try to challenge the next windmill.

The principal was polite but reserved. She again explained the admission requirement for Pre-K, hoping I would shuffle off to the parking lot and let her get on with her day. When I explained that Michael hadn't had the early nurturing he needed from his birth parents and foster care, her expression changed completely.

"Are you adopting Michael?"

"Yes, we're trying. It's pending in the courts, but we have custody, so we're authorized to do things like enrolling him in school."

She pointed to a picture of a handsome young teen on her desk. "That's my son, Jimmy. He's adopted too!"

That's when I learned there is an instant universal connection between adoptive parents.

She pulled out some forms and handed them to me. "Fill out these forms and I'll sign them. Michael will start Pre-K here in August, and he will have speech therapy every week." This lady had clout and compassion.

So how did it turn out that the principal for our zoned school was an adoptive Mom? She had been the principal there for many years, ready and waiting for us when needed. I guess this was God's way of assuring us that He was still working on our case.

Chapter Twelve
IN THE BEST INTEREST

After months of nail biting, the day arrived for our next hearing. Now we were arguing both custody and jurisdiction for the case. We had a new judge who was fresh to this jumble of issues. We were all seated at a table in front of the judge. He tried to keep the hearing informal, advising the attorneys there was no need to stand when they spoke. Every time the tribe's attorney spoke, he stood up and was very crisp and formal. When the judge gently reminded him that it was unnecessary, he replied, "Sorry judge. I'm used to trying cases in Federal court."

No doubt he was trying to impress the judge and intimidate our attorney. It backfired completely, by insulting and demeaning the judge instead. He probably felt like he had just been reduced to someone perched on a hay bale. Not a Norman Vincent Peale moment. *Strike one!* The judge spent a lot of time trying to clarify our position. How were we related? How old were the boys and how were they acclimating to living with us? What had we done to provide any special care for them?

Each time he asked a question concerning the boys' welfare, the tribe's attorney stood and objected that the focus should remain on the issue of jurisdiction. The judge grizzled more and more. *Strike two!*

After hearing all the testimony it was pretty clear the judge was ready to rule in our favor. Up popped the tribe's attorney one final time.

"Judge, the best interest of the children is *not* to be an issue in this case."

"Well, it is in MY court!" *Strike 3. You're out!*

The judge retreated to his chambers for a short while for a final review. He came back with a decision in our favor. We gasped a sigh of relief! The tribe's attorney immediately stated the case would be appealed up to the District court. *End of game.*

We learned a new term—ad litem. The judge now appointed two ad litem attorneys to the case. Because Michael had a different legal status than Mark and Matthew, he had a separate attorney to represent his interests. Another attorney was appointed to represent Mark and Matthew. So now there were four attorneys embroiled in this battle! How complicated could that get?

Chapter Thirteen

PHONE BOOKS ARE BETTER THAN THE INTERNET

T rying to keep focused on work was becoming more and more difficult. I needed more firepower. There was a Christian radio station on the same floor of our office building. I walked by it every day, but had never had any reason to stop in. Wiping away tears in the Ladies Room, I decided it was time to venture in.

I went up to the receptionist and told her I was going through a difficult time. I asked if there was someone who could pray with me. It was awkward asking that of a complete stranger, but I figured this was as close to a church as it gets, so it wasn't completely off base.

An employee came out very quickly and invited me into her office. She asked what was happening and then listened as I tried to trim it down to 100 words or less. Technical issues aside, she definitely saw this was a David and Goliath situation, and we needed a slingshot. She prayed with me and told me not to worry. God would move mountains for us. Of course, she had no answers. I wasn't really looking for any from her. I just needed another prayer sister. How wonderful that they happened to be next door!

I had a phone message from her later that day. Another pink message slip, and the phone number wasn't very legible. I knew the station's call letters and pulled out the business phone book. (Some of you may have to ask someone older to explain that.)

I started scrolling through the K's. KAQZ? KBRC? Which one was it? Then my eyes darted to a listing in bright red capital letters just above the K's.

JUSTICE FOR CHILDREN

I had no idea what that was, but God did everything except put lights on it. Pretty sure I was supposed to call them. The internet wouldn't have done that. Score one for us old-school folks.

I called the number and sheepishly said I had no idea what they did and would like some information. I was told that they advocated in cases where children were at risk in family court cases. She invited me to meet with her and give her more information about our case. Once again, I tried to figure out how to explain all of this to a total stranger and make some sort of sense of it. She was very empathetic and said she would talk with her team to see how they might be able to help. I hoped to hear back soon.

Later, I decided to just go to the radio station and see why they called. They were very excited and told me they had a talk show in their daily format. They wanted to interview me on the air to discuss the situation with the boys. I didn't see how it could help, but didn't see any downside either, so I agreed.

The interview went reasonably well. I was nervous and awkward, but that probably helped it come across as real and unrehearsed. At any rate, it was good to be heard. Hopefully, this would increase our prayer warrior team. It was definitely building.

Another message from the radio station.

They had been contacted by a reporter with the Houston Post who heard the interview. She wanted to meet with me to learn more and put a story in the paper. I doubted it would happen but agreed to meet with her.

We had a good visit together and seemed to connect well. I felt if anything did get printed, it would be to our benefit. It never hurts to get the public on your side, even if it's buried in the personal columns. She called back a few days later and said her editor wanted to send out a photographer to get a shot of us together. I was surprised at that but agreed. Wanting to get some natural shots of a family in their normal routine, they showed up at 7:00 in the morning. They got natural habitat! The selected photo showed me dressed with wet hair and no make-up, struggling to get three boys dressed. Not going to grace the cover of Vogue.

Chapter Fourteen
FIFTEEN MINUTES OF FAME

D ays passed and we heard nothing further. We checked the daily papers and didn't find anything. The editor must have decided to pass on the article. We didn't really expect anything to come of it anyway. A little cultural history may be needed here for some readers. At the risk of sounding ancient, back then the Sunday paper was a huge deal. Everybody got the Sunday paper! It was actually a paper, not online, and it had everything.

Families would dash to get their favorite section. The biggest fight was always over the funnies. That glorious full color menagerie of our favorite comic strips was savored. Would Charlie Brown finally kick the football? What crisis would give Cathy a meltdown? Would Odie manage to trump Garfield for a change? How would dashing Prince Valiant rescue his beloved wife, Queen Aleta?

There was a mega-load of coupons to be scoured and clipped for the week's grocery shopping. I have to admit downloading them on my computer today is much easier and faster, but there was something captivating about seeking each bargain. Scissors flew into action every Sunday. For those in search of new or better jobs, the Sunday Employment section had all the new job listings. Many employers only put an ad in the Sunday paper. It was a world of opportunity at your ink-smudged fingertips.

And there was Parade Magazine. This insert had all the current dope on movie stars, health trends, and politicians. Always something of interest for curious readers. All the grocery and drug stores had newsstands, and the Sunday paper was always there in abundance. People who didn't subscribe would stop to get the massive edition to take home for the afternoon entertainment. Something of common interest was always flashed all over the front page to give a little extra insurance of selling every last copy.

I stopped at the grocery store after church the next Sunday and was jolted to a stop when I passed the news stand at the entrance. There we were, in glorious color, on the front page! The common interest story was US! The article took up two pages of the Sunday edition. Apparently, the editor liked our story. Monday morning my phone rang non-stop. Every Houston TV station wanted an interview! I called my attorney and he said to go ahead. It wasn't exactly top secret after the Sunday paper went out.

That afternoon we had reporters from all three TV stations in our home at once. It was total bedlam, but the boys were loving the excitement. The reporters went around our living room putting microphones to our faces and asking questions. Suddenly Matthew worked his way through the crowd holding a toy microphone he had gotten in a Happy Meal. He lifted it up to me to be part of the action. Everyone fell out laughing and it made it onto the air. Surely, we had completely maxed out our 15 minutes of fame. Apparently not.

A couple of weeks later, NBC Nightly News picked up on it and again sent reporters and photographers to our home. The boys were now media pros. The competition to be center stage was brutal. Each one managed to find something that produced an "awwwww" moment. When Mark spun around in a circle creating a giant bubble that swarmed around his head like a halo, the camera man surrendered.

"Can you ask them not to do anything else that's cute?"

I wasn't sure whether all the sweetness was edging his blood sugar up or if he was running low on film. Either way, he was done. They also interviewed some of the tribal members in Arizona to get their point of view.

It was actually very helpful to us to understand their position better. Instead of just meeting an attorney, now we were seeing a very kind woman who had also adopted two little girls needing a home and a family. They were from another tribe, and she wanted to make sure they didn't lose their Native American identity. That had always been important to us too. Maybe we could find some common ground after all.

Chapter Fifteen

THE OLIVE BRANCH

We finally had some information on the boys' tribe thanks to the interview on NBC. Yvette had never talked about them. All we knew was that they were somewhere in Arizona. That didn't narrow it down much. We always felt if we could just open the lines of communication with the tribe, we would be able to reach an understanding and work things out. The legal fees on both sides were piling up and seemed like a huge waste of money that should have been used to care for the boys. I know we spent at least one college tuition.

Beyond the frugal side of the matter, we truly wanted them to learn about both sides of their heritage. Charlie was not just an avid reader; he devoured books and scoured the bargains at the used bookstores every week. He had put all of the managers on notice to hold any books on Native American culture and history that came into the store. Soon we had a collection that could rival a university.

We talked with the boys often about it and went to every event we could find that included Native American dancers and culture. Still, we really wanted to work things out so they could visit their tribe and meet relatives on that side of the family.

I decided to write to their tribe and try to open a dialogue. I explained that we weren't trying to take the boys away from the tribe and how we were related to them. My handwriting hadn't improved since the first grade, so I typed it to make sure they could read everything. I sent pictures and information on everything they were doing. I dug through packets of photos from school, doctors, church, our house, and backyard with a swing set. I found out the name of the tribal chairman and addressed a very large envelope to his attention. We prayed it would be well received.

Time passed without any response. Then we received a large white envelope from the tribe. I was so excited I could barely open it. My heart sank when it contained our envelope––unopened. Phone calls were also to no avail. We spoke with a very understanding receptionist but were never able to get any further. She finally told us as kindly as possible to stop wasting our money on long distance calls. She wished us well and quietly told me she was praying for us. There would be no trip to meet with them and get to know each other. Just the next court date.

Chapter Sixteen
DISTRICT COURT REUNION

We had no way to talk with Yvette about the case. She had left Houston, and we had no idea how to reach her. It turned out the tribe had flown her back to the reservation. Then we were very surprised to see that they flew her back to Houston to appear in our District court hearing. We had a good relationship with Yvette when she had stayed with us in the past.

Here's a little family history for you. A few years earlier, Terry had called and told me they were homeless and staying at a local mission. I went to pick everyone up and take them to live with us until they could get on their feet. They just had Michael and Mark then. Terry found work in San Antonio, and they found an apartment. He told us everything was ready for Yvette and the boys to live there.

We drove them to their new home and found a mattress on the floor and a very empty refrigerator and pantry. We drove to the nearest grocery store and loaded up the cart. It broke our hearts to leave the boys there, but we had done all we could. A few weeks later I got a call from Yvette. She was sick with the flu, Terry was in jail, and they were being evicted. *Back to San Antonio.*

With everyone loaded into the car, we headed back to Houston. On the way, she told me she was pregnant. I'm not sure how I avoided screaming expletives, or driving into the back of a semi, but angels apparently restrained me. She was sick with the flu, so I put her to bed and got the kids fed, bathed, and tucked in for the night.

When she recovered, I sat with her and asked why she hadn't used the birth control pills I had provided. I had taken her to Planned Parenthood before driving her back to San Antonio. She said it was too hard to take them. I lost it for a minute and blurted out, "How could you get pregnant again when you can't afford to care for the kids you have?

She looked at me like I had been living in a cave. "The government will take care of them!" *End of conversation.*

When she got back on her feet, I helped her get a job at a fast-food restaurant near the house. We all helped watch the boys so she could work. She was able to save up most of her money to start a nest egg for the baby. Then my nephew, Terry, came to stay with us too. It wasn't long before old addictions took over both of them. Soon they stormed out with Michael and Mark because they couldn't live with our rules. I'm omitting their adjectives for the faint of heart.

Our unreasonable rules had been a midnight curfew, so we weren't awakened in the middle of the night, and not taking the boys out in the middle of the night on their *errands.* They found a friend at Yvette's work who would take them in. Terry came to pick up the clothes and toys. We asked several times for him to let us know where they were going, or at least give us a phone number, so we could help if there was an emergency. When I asked a final time, I got an expletive coated rejection.

I have no recollection of what followed. Charlie loved telling how I jumped up, grabbed the big black trash bag filled with toys and clothes, and swung it at Terry, knocking him out the open front doorway. Then he grabbed the bag, jumped into the waiting car and they sped off. Not my finest moment.

Within a few months, I was in the resale shop buying that baby afghan for Matthew. We hoped to get a chance to talk with Yvette before the hearing started. Maybe our efforts in the past would help her to see we were doing what was best for the boys. The tribe's attorney made sure that didn't come to pass.

We had been able to reach Terry and asked him to sign a document saying he wanted the boys to stay with us and that he wanted jurisdiction to stay in the Texas courts. That might at least help with Mark and Matthew. But it left Michael hanging out in the wind. His ad litem attorney was going to have to fight for him.

When Yvette took the stand, she told the judge how much she wanted the boys back and that she would do anything to be able to do that. The judge was clearly concerned that sobriety was not included in that. He was not comfortable with the idea of taking that chance. Michael's ad litem attorney asked her if she would want to keep Michael if we kept Mark and Matthew. She answered that she wanted the boys to stay together no matter how things worked out. She didn't want them to be separated. She had been separated from her siblings as a child in multiple foster homes and didn't want that happening to the boys.

We waited to see which way the decision would go. I could feel all of our prayer warriors helping us breathe. After what seemed an eternity, the judge gave his decision. Jurisdiction would remain in Harris County and the boys would stay with us. We were ecstatic with the ruling, but we also felt great empathy for Yvette. We were finally able to talk with her and trade some Kleenex and hugs. She understood we weren't trying to hurt her. We just wanted the boys to have a secure home. She told us she was grateful and knew they were going to be okay with us.

Yvette went back to Arizona. We never saw her again. We thought the battle was finally over. For a few weeks, we felt like a normal family. Avoiding stepping on building blocks with bare feet was our biggest anxiety. Then came the next large white envelope. We had a date with the Texas Supreme Court—I was starting to develop a phobia about large white envelopes.

Chapter Seventeen
PRO BONO ANYONE?

Remember that lady at **Justice for Children**? You've probably forgotten about her by now. But she hadn't forgotten about us. She called me and said they were going to have a meeting with young attorneys who were interested in doing some pro bono work on family law cases. She asked if they could present our case and see if anyone might be interested. It was a long shot, but one worth taking.

She followed up the next day with excitement in her voice. One of the attorneys asked her to give us his contact information. He wanted to set up a meeting to find out more about our case and consider representing us! Interesting thing about that meeting. His wife had heard about it and urged him to go with her. They were both right out of law school and working with their first law firms. He had agreed but was tired that evening and tried to beg off. She wasn't having it. She insisted they were going to the meeting, and he reluctantly went to preserve harmony at home. God bless her!

We met for lunch and tried to present a synopsis of everything that had come to pass. Not an easy task. After hearing everything he leaned forward and asked just one question. "Are you completely committed to this? I have to know that if I take on the case you won't decide to back out when things get tough."

"Of course! They're our kids now. There's no way we could ever walk away from them!"

He gave a satisfied nod and explained he would need to give his law firm time to check for any possible conflicts of interest. If they gave him the green light, he would take over the case—pro bono!

By this time our finances were exhausted. Our savings were gone, and our credit cards were maxed out from all of the legal fees and expenses for the boys. Medical bills were piling up too. Charlie's health was being affected by all of the stress. He didn't just take the boys into his home. He took them into his heart. He couldn't bear the thought of them being shuffled off to live with strangers.

We had no way to pay the costs of a legal battle in the Texas Supreme Court. Without his help, we would have lost the boys by default. We got our prayer team in overdrive. Thank God for bad handwriting and the phone book!

Chapter Eighteen

SCOTT WITH WHOM???

A few weeks later I got a call from Scott. His firm had given him the green light to take on the case pro bono. They were behind it with their full support! I hoped my shriek of delight didn't burst his eardrum. He said *they* would start working on it right away. Someone from the *team* would keep me posted on their progress and let me know if they needed anything from us.

They were Fulbright and Jaworski, one of the premier law firms in the country! He hadn't mentioned that. This was going to end up being an incredible team effort by countless attorneys poring over every aspect of the case. They weren't just agreeing to work on it. They were passionate about it!

Please allow a moment of digression here. When my sister and I were children, our mother announced that she was going to have a new baby. She asked us to pray very hard for a boy. Eventually the big day came and our brother, Chris, was brought home. That should have been the end of that prayer chain. But 18 months later she also brought home our brother, Bob.

I was a bit put off by it all and my mother was concerned. She put her arms around me and asked, "Don't you like your new little brother?"

I shrugged and replied, "He's okay."

"Then what's wrong?"

"Remember when you were going to have a baby and we all prayed for a boy,

and we got Chris?"

"Yes."

"Well, somebody prayed too hard because we got two!"

My grandmother flew out of the room leaving my mother to deal with it.

Anyway, I tell that story because I feel the same way now. We were all praying for an attorney to take over our case pro bono. Somebody definitely prayed too hard because we got a whole team of them! Sure glad his wife dragged him to that meeting!

Chapter Nineteen
ICWA

The yo-yo effect seemed to apply as much to our case as to dieting. Every time we moved forward, we got pushed ten steps back. The tribe's attorney kept referring to federal laws that applied to jurisdiction. No one was well versed in that area, so we kept getting out maneuvered in court—until. Scott dug into it and discovered ICWA, the Indian Child Welfare Act.

The purpose of this Act is very understandable. For decades, Native American children had been placed in the homes of white families by authorities. They lost their cultural identity and their tribes frequently lost contact with them. Dwindling tribal roles affected both government funding and their very survival as a people. The Act would give jurisdiction over placement to the tribal courts.

This was a very different situation. We were related to the boys, not just some random family who received placement by a government entity. We wanted them to retain their cultural identity and hoped to be able to visit the tribe with them once everything was worked out. But this was a very tough law to challenge.

Scott called a few weeks later and was very excited. His firm had recently hired a new attorney, also straight out of law school. Her final paper had been on the Indian Child Welfare Act! This wasn't a breadcrumb. It was a whole loaf! She advised us that we could not win by focusing on the welfare of the children. The only way to keep the case in the Texas courts was to submit written, notarized, statements of objection to transfer of jurisdiction from one of the birth parents. Without that, we were building ice castles in the desert.

We had the objection from Terry, which could protect Mark and Matthew. But Michael's birth father was unknown. Yvette did not give us any way to contact her. So, we were stuck in our efforts to keep the boys together. His ad litem attorney put notices in the San Antonio newspaper, where Michael was born. No luck. There was no one to object to transfer of jurisdiction for Michael.

I was talking with Scott about it and a lightning bolt hit me. (Sometimes God can be very loud when He speaks.) I approached him with the message that was ringing in my ears.

"Scott, I was always lousy in math. But I remember one thing. If A = B and B = C, then A = C."

Blank stare.

"We have the objection to transfer for Mark and Matthew. We have testimony in court from Yvette saying that she wants the boys to stay together. She said whatever happens with Mark and Matthew, she wants the same to be for Michael."

Nod.

"Doesn't that give us Yvette's objection to transfer for Michael by default?"

Scott looked like one of the old "Big Eyes" paintings. Pretty sure he heard the thunder. He said he would go back and talk to the senior partners about the idea. We may have found our "Hail Mary" play.

God bless Sister Zoe! I drove her crazy in the ninth grade. At the first parent-teacher conference, she told my mother that she didn't know how to grade my Algebra papers. I got the right answers but got them the wrong way. Instead of using the formulas, I took detours and U-turns to reach my destination. At least she managed to teach my math-challenged brain that much!

Chapter Twenty

TEXAS SUPREME COURT, THE DUKE, AND PSALM 23

T he day had finally arrived to present our case to the Texas Supreme Court. All of our prayer warriors were lined up, as well as TV reporters from all the networks. We said a prayer, gulped a deep breath, and found our seats. Hopefully you have never had this experience, and never will. Here is how it works. There isn't any testimony. The three Supreme Court Justices seated at the front of the room have already spent considerable time reviewing all the prior courts' transcripts. They have also reviewed the briefs filed by the attorneys on both sides. Now it's time for short opening statements followed by nerve-racking "Q&A" between the Justices and the attorneys. Then final closing statements come from the attorneys, and everyone leaves. Talk about a cliffhanger!

Unknown to any of the participants, I had brought a secret weapon. It was a book on the 23rd Psalm. I had worn the pages as thin as rice paper, but it was still legible. Every time the tribe's attorney stood up to talk, I silently prayed it over and over and over. A very strange thing happened. He had always been smooth as a polished stone and serenely confident in court. As he had often mentioned, he was no stranger to federal courts, so this state court should not have jangled his demeanor. But every time he spoke, he stumbled around like a lawyer arguing his first case. Nothing came out right. He struggled to remember the names of cases he wanted to reference. Everything was scrambled and he kept going blank. He frantically tore through his notes trying to find the needed details. The look on his face was incredulous. *What on earth is happening to me?*

I recalled an episode of the Tonight Show back in the days of Johnny Carson. George Goebel was a guest and was talking about being in awkward situations. He asked Johnny, "Did you ever feel like a pair of brown shoes in a world full of tuxedos?" That always stayed with me, and I kept looking to see if he might be wearing brown shoes with that gray suit. I'm sure he felt that way. It was all I could do to avoid a smirk. I knew exactly what, or better *Who*, was happening.

Scott and his partners had decided that my Algebra argument indeed had merit. It became the basis of their argument. Did I bless Sister Zoe yet? I hope so. The tribe's attorney said that the objection to transfer of jurisdiction by "some Johnny-come-lately father" should not be applicable. Big mistake—HUGE! When it was Scott's turn to speak, he sauntered up to the podium like The Duke. All that was missing was a white hat and a trusty six-shooter.

"The only 'Johnny come lately' here is the tribe! Where were they when these children were homeless and hungry? The Jenkins are the ones who came to their aid and took care of them. Their birth father knows they will have the best possible care with them, and that's why he submitted his objection to transfer of jurisdiction with the court." Great shooting even by Texas standards. Then he went into the argument to include Michael in the objection to transfer by default. He was more technical than I was with my math formula. It was nicely polished in legal jargon, but we all got the point.

One of the Justices asked the tribe's attorney a question about ICWA. He inquired about the definition in the law about who could object to transfer of jurisdiction. He addressed the tribe's attorney.

"Does the law say, 'good father' or just 'father'?"

"It says *father*," was the reluctant and sheepish reply.

To shoot himself in the other foot, he stated that Native American children could not be properly raised by a white family. It would be detrimental to their well-being. One of the Justices looked like he needed to squeeze a stress ball—as hard as possible. We found out much later that he was Native American and had been adopted by white parents. It seemed he didn't turn out too badly.

I lost track of time, but the hearing seemed to go on for hours. My book was just about worn to shreds. I probably didn't need it anyway. Surely that psalm was memorized by now, even for someone who had only retained one formula from a year of Algebra. It was finally over. The attorneys talked with the reporters, and we did our best to avoid it. We just wanted to breathe.

Scott felt it all went quite well. He seemed bewildered by his opponent's presentation. I saw no reason to explain. He told us this wasn't like the movies. It would probably be several months before the Justices would render their decision. Time to just focus on the boys and put it out of our minds.

Sure! No problem.

We had been instructed not to say anything to any of the Justices if we encountered them. As we were walking down a corridor toward the exit, all three of them were walking together toward us. The temptation to speak was grueling, but we managed to just give them a meek smile as we were passing by. They all gave us a big smile, as if to say, "Don't worry. *We've got this.*"

Chapter Twenty-One
HIS AUTOGRAPH

S cott was right. It was several months of watching an hourglass waiting to hear a final decision from the Texas Supreme Court. We had to just acknowledge that it was in God's hands in order to keep our sanity. Charlie had more difficulty with that. He wasn't exactly an agnostic, but he struggled greatly with faith. He wanted to release his doubts and fully surrender but hadn't been able to make the leap.

When we finally got temporary custody of the boys, we asked our pastor to baptize them. Charlie told me he had never been baptized, which was surprising knowing how strong his mother was in her faith. He decided to be baptized with them. We teased our pastor about getting a group rate. They all lined up at the baptismal font. Our pastor asked who should go first. Charlie said he should, so he could show the boys that it didn't hurt. Even with Father Jim's many years of experience, I don't think he had heard that one before.

The boys followed his lead and grinned when they received a major ovation from the pews. They weren't sure what it was all about, but being the center of attention never hurts. Of course, the strongest faith can still flounder when the situation is stressful enough. Peter certainly proved that more than once. Charlie still felt the need to tightly clench the steering wheel.

When he would start to worry and talk about what else we could do about the case, I would smile and take his hand. I'd do my best to reassure him that God had this in His control, and all would end up as He intended. One evening he was tired and overwrought. My response caused him to blow up.

"I've had it with your Pollyanna attitude!"

Before I could weigh my words, I blurted back, "He gave us Fulbright and Jaworski. What do you need––His autograph?!"

Dead silence.

I went to bed and left him to stew on it for a while. This may not seem like much, but in 10 years of marriage we had never raised voices to each other. Honest. The words seemed to shoot out from me like a ventriloquist's dummy.

The next day I overheard him on the phone while I was fixing dinner. He was calling everyone he knew and telling them all about our MIRACLE with Fulbright and Jaworski! He knew everything was going to be okay now. I had never heard Charlie use the word miracle before in that way. He would say things like it was a miracle the dog never bit the boys the way they wrestled with him, and stuff like that. But a real, genuine, Grade A miracle? This was new.

I felt in my heart that Charlie had finally managed to make the final leap. I stopped feeling bad about yelling at him the night before. I knew those words didn't come from me. I think he did too. The gift of Fulbright and Jaworski was tremendous. The gift of faith for Charlie was a pearl beyond price. Sure glad Scott went to law school when he grew up.

Chapter Twenty-Two
A WOMAN'S TOUCH

Afteter what seemed an eternity, we finally heard from Scott. He could barely contain himself as he told us that the Texas Supreme Court had upheld jurisdiction in the Texas courts. Our case would not be moved to the tribal court. We could finally proceed with our request for adoption! But our elation was short-lived. A few days later we got a second call from Scott. The tribe was going to appeal again––to the U. S. Supreme Court. Mind blown.

Scott told us his firm needed him on another case, but they were going to stay with us to the end. They had assigned our case to another attorney. She had more experience, and he felt she would actually be better suited to handle the case from this point forward. We didn't know how to take the news. On one hand, we were incredibly grateful that Fulbright and Jaworski were still willing to stay with us on this case. We couldn't imagine what kind of costs would be involved if this went all the way to the Supreme Court.

On the other hand, Scott was our hero. He had taken on our case and believed in it with all his heart. He didn't hold any punches when it counted in court. If John Wayne had become a lawyer, he would have been a mirror of Scott. How could anyone be better? Of course, God always knows what we need long before we do. It turned out that Scott was with us when we needed a cowboy. Now it was time for a new approach. Mediation might just keep this from heading to Washington. It would take a different style to pull it off. Gentle, but firm, persuasion was the new course.

When we met with Terriann, we could see that she was just as tough as Scott. She just had a way of softening her approach. She was a Steel Magnolia, definitely not someone I would want to go up against. I thought about the old saying that Ginger Rogers had to do everything that Fred Astaire did. But she had to do it backward and in high heels. She was also an adoptive Mom who understood every gut-wrenching fear that kept us awake at night. And she understood that adoptive parents love their kids just as much as natural parents. And they would fight just as hard to protect them.

Terriann managed to find a good mediator for a case with so many points of view and so much at stake. And she got everyone to come to the table. I have no idea how she pulled that off. Charlie and I spent the day in a small room at the mediator's office. All we could do was wait for Terriann to come back with updates. We had no opportunity to have any dialogue. It was all between the attorneys.

After several hours, she came back with a final question. Would we consider just having custody of the boys, but not adoption? This is one of those fear vs. faith moments. You have to pick one and go with it. At first, we started to cave in with fear. Could we really risk rolling the dice on all or nothing? Maybe we should give in to just having custody. At least it would all finally be over.

But then again, stopping short of adoption, would the boys really be safe? Could it all start up again if a new tribal council decided to pursue it? Faith was the only way to go. We decided that we had to believe that after God had taken us this far, He would not abandon us now. We had to insist on full adoption for all three boys. Terriann wasn't surprised at our decision. I think she had more faith in us than we had in ourselves. She told them there was no middle ground on the point of adoption. The tribe's attorney would need to relay the impasse to the tribal council.

As we were getting ready to leave, the mediator came into the room where we had been sitting, and sweating, all day. He told us he did all he could, but he could tell early on that it was pointless. He relayed that the tribe's attorney had told him the boys would be better off with the worst Native American family than with the best white family. Not very promising for finding a middle ground.

That was when we finally understood that everything we had been doing for the boys was meaningless in his eyes. That was not the issue. To him, they simply did not belong in our home or our lives. We could only imagine the report he would take back to the tribal council.

Chapter Twenty-Three
REMEMBER DR. BRUCE?

T he boys continued meeting with Dr. Bruce and his staff through the years. They made good progress, but still needed some help, especially Michael. His trust issues continued to affect his behavior and interactions with us. During this time, we got a surprising call from Terriann. The tribal council was not satisfied with the way the mediation turned out. They were sending three members to Houston to meet with us. Not with a mediator. Not with an attorney. With US!

This was what we had always hoped for. We always felt if we could just sit down and talk to each other, we could work things out so the boys could have a secure home and family and still retain their cultural heritage. We were ecstatic! Just one problem. Where could we find neutral ground for the meeting?

Paging Dr. Bruce!

His office was the perfect neutral ground. It also gave the tribal members a chance to see the boys with the case workers in a room full of toys, totally unaware of the importance of this visit. Dr. Bruce was happy to work as a mediator with all of us in his conference room.

We all arrived at his office at the same time. We awkwardly smiled at each other as we stepped out of the elevators. There was a man and two women. I was particularly taken by one of the women. She somehow radiated a spirit of warmth and had a sense of calm strength about her. She proudly wore Native American jewelry, not in a showy way, but as part of her identity. Everything about her seemed very natural and comfortable.

We were ushered into the conference room while they had an opportunity to view the boys. This was the first time they had seen them, and it seemed to mean a lot to them to finally have that chance. Little did I know how much. I hope you didn't forget that I mentioned earlier that Dr. Bruce had some special skills. Well, here's another one of those mega crumbs. It turns out that Dr. Bruce had spent a few years working with the Cree Nation. He had done a lot of counseling for their children and was very highly respected among Native American tribes for that work. Talk about having street cred! We had no idea of that experience. Dr. Bruce had never mentioned it to us. But it may be part of the reason he was so interested in working with the boys. He had much more to share with them than we imagined.

Eventually he entered the room with the council members and their attorney. We were sitting with Terriann, and all offered the best smiles we could muster. Dr. Bruce had already gone a big way toward making them feel comfortable. This wasn't some Ivy League white guy who wouldn't understand how they felt. He was the perfect mediator for us. Of course, God knew that a long time ago. At first their conversation and questions were very guarded. I took the lead in addressing them. It was a Mom thing. Terriann sat back and let the communication build. She could see it was going in the right direction.

Most of the conversation was with Theresa, the woman who

had impressed me so much with her demeanor. The other woman remained silent throughout our meeting but listened very intently to every word. I felt God telling me for several days leading up to our meeting that it was important to stay fully positive. Nothing derogatory should be said about Yvette. Instead, we should focus on how we tried to help her before ending up needing to take in the boys. We needed to show empathy, not judgment.

Eventually the tribal member named Vincent explained why they had been chosen by the tribal council to attend the meeting. It turned out that Vincent and Mary, the silent member, were Yvette's aunt and uncle! None of us had any idea that they were related. Apparently, there's a lot of wisdom in that Scripture about seasoning your words with salt.

He asked us how they would be treated if they came to visit. Without time to think, I reacted from the heart. I told him they would be treated like family. That was what they were. They both seemed very pleased. Then we were advised that Theresa was a very important member of the council. She was also the adoptive Mom we had seen on that NBC National News report so many months back. We hadn't made the connection. She wanted to see if this was just an issue for us, or if we truly had the boys in our hearts.

Vincent commented that he wished we could have done this sooner. Then it wouldn't have become such a big legal mess. With another dose of salt on my tongue, I calmly explained that we had tried from the beginning to open dialogue with the tribe. I told them about the long letter and envelope filled with pictures and information about the boys that was sent to the tribe years back.

They had never been told about it and were taken aback. I

explained that it was returned unopened and that shortly after we received the notice of the suit being filed.

"Who did you send it to?"

"We sent it to Ted Weathers." (The name is changed for obvious reasons).

Mary, who had been silent for the entire meeting, suddenly slammed her hand down on the table.

"Oh Ted! That's my brother. He's an idiot!"

I guess every family has its dissension. A laugh all around opened the door to comfortable conversation.

The tribe's attorney was really scowling by now. He saw that we were moving toward a meeting of the minds and his visions of his day at the US Supreme Court were quickly vanishing. Every time we would start making progress, he would try to throw a monkey wrench into the conversation to block it.

Theresa locked eyes on me and said, "It seems like every time we move a step forward, the lawyers drag us two steps back. Do we need attorneys in this room?" I glanced quickly at Terriann. She was smiling.

"I don't," was my response.

Theresa motioned to their attorney to leave, and Terriann quickly moved to the door.

Her attorney not only didn't move, but he actually seemed to block the door. It was time to head for the one place he couldn't follow us. To the Ladies Room! Theresa motioned to me, and I followed her. With a subtle grin, she led me to no-man's land.

It still amazes me that two caring women could resolve a four-year legal battle in five minutes in the Ladies Room, but that's exactly how it went down. The boys would be enrolled as tribal members and we would be allowed to adopt them. We would all be welcome to visit in Arizona at any time, and their family would always be welcome to visit us.

We returned to the conference room with Theresa advising that everything was settled, and it was time to leave. For the first time, we felt able to take a deep breath. How did we get in to see a top child psychiatrist with a waiting list a mile long, who just *happened* to have a history of working with Native American children? And thank the Lord that the tribe selected a male attorney who couldn't follow us into the Ladies Room!

Chapter Twenty-Four
IN GOD'S GOOD TIME

A t last, we could see the light at the end of the tunnel. Our four-year legal battle was over. There were no more objections to adopting the boys. The tribe sent us the tribal enrollment forms, and we quickly completed and returned them. We were glad to know they would be added to the tribal roles and have that part of their heritage secured. They would always be able to trace back their Native American roots. They could also participate in tribal ceremonies and traditions.

There was a major cultural heritage celebration in Arizona every spring called Exodus Day. We were all invited to attend and participate. The boys would have a wonderful introduction! I mentioned a while back that all the stress had taken its toll on Charlie's health. Even with insurance, our portion of the medical expenses were several thousand dollars. Between the medical bills and the legal bills, we had no choice but to file for bankruptcy.

We wanted to take the boys to Arizona, but there was no spare change left in the cookie jar. Without even asking, the tribe told us they would be paying for our airfare and motel stay. It was a great load off our minds. We would be able to make the trip that would finally meld us into one family. The celebration was a few months after the scheduled adoption, so the timing was perfect.

Charlie was now on kidney dialysis and needed to have it done three times a week. He worked out the treatment schedule so there wouldn't be any conflict with our trip. We lined up vacation time from work for the final adoption hearing and our trip. All systems GO! About a week before the final adoption hearing, Charlie needed to have a minor outpatient procedure done for his dialysis treatment. Without getting technical, it was sort of a Roto Rooter situation so the dialysis would work smoothly. It had to be completed periodically, and we were used to it being done. No big deal.

He normally had it done as an outpatient and then went back to work or came home, depending on what time he finished. The procedure was completed late in the day, and he was quite tired, so the doctor agreed to have him stay overnight. Then he could have his dialysis done first thing the next morning. About 2:00 in the morning the phone rang. Charlie wasn't coming home. I don't remember much after that. Everything went into a blur. I just remember being numb.

The next morning, I didn't tell the boys. I got them off to school and day care as usual. I wasn't prepared to try to break the news to them. I met my pastor at the hospital. He had spent time there as the hospital's Chaplain, so knew the procedures. I was so grateful for his guidance and support. After spending some time together in the chapel, we went to sign the necessary formal paperwork. It still didn't seem real.

When I got home, I called Dr. Bruce's office and let them know what had happened. They gave me advice on how to talk with the boys and offered to have us come to their office so they could help. I managed to somehow explain it to them when they got home that day. It took a few days for them to digest it. In the midst of all this, a chilling thought hit me. This had just become a single parent adoption. Would this change everything? Would the maze start all over again? Would the tribe's attorney decide to challenge it? I called Terriann and told her in a very shaken voice what had happened. Not an easy phone call for either of us. She told me not to worry and contacted the myriad of attorneys involved. There would be no challenge. The adoption would proceed as scheduled.

For several days dinner kept arriving at our door. A friend at church organized it for us. The last thing I could think about was fixing dinner, but the boys needed to eat. I was so grateful for their kindness. Without them, it would have been a lot of peanut butter and Cheetos for a while. The odd thing was that several well-meaning people asked me if I was still going to go ahead with the adoption. I know they were concerned about how I would be able to handle everything, but it seemed bizarre to even ask the question. I certainly wasn't going to abandon the boys after loving and raising them for four years just because it wasn't convenient now. I just managed a minimal smile and assured them that nothing had changed.

Charlie was buried in Georgia in their family plot. That meant the boys didn't have to endure a funeral with a casket. It was just a beautiful memorial service at our church with everyone cherishing his memory and laughing at the humor he always shared so freely. It was truly a blessing to all of us.

As the adoption hearing approached, I suddenly felt like I couldn't handle it alone. I called my pastor and told him that Charlie had been with me at every hearing. It would be such an empty feeling not having him standing there beside me. I asked him if he would consider attending and standing in his place. There was a short pause.

"I'd be honored" was his humble response.

So, adoption day finally came. The boys were dressed in their Sunday best. I wore slacks instead of my usual suit, knowing they would be climbing all over me while we were waiting to go before the judge. Better safe than sorry.

All of the attorneys offered hugs and condolences. To my surprise, the tribe's attorney offered them too. I could see he was touched by the situation and truly cared.

When we went before the judge, he asked to go off the record for a moment.

"Mrs. Jenkins, I know we have had to be adversaries, but it was just the way things had to be done. I want you to know …" I could see he was struggling for words. I gave him a smile and reached out my hand.

"It's cool, Fernando."

His appreciation was visible on his face. When we went back on the record, his demeanor was much softer than I had ever seen it.

After the formalities were completed, the judge gave us all a huge smile. He said most of the time in family court his work was difficult and often very sad. He was so glad to have a happy ending for a change. He asked us to come up and take a photo with him. We crowded around him, and he pulled Matthew onto his lap. He could have retired a very happy man at that moment.

It was finally done! We all shared the same last name. No more sleepless nights wondering what legal assault would come next.

Just peace—at least as much as a single Mom with three little boys would find possible. We had pleasant things to look forward to now. There would be an adoption blessing at our church, and the trip to Arizona was coming up in a few weeks.

I wished Charlie could have gone with us. But I saw God's perfect timing. We would be grieving for some time, but the trip would help to start pulling us forward. It was something fun and exciting that could pierce the gloom and give us a much-needed break. He knew what we would need, and when we would need it.

Chapter Twenty-Five

ADOPTION BLESSING

T here was one step remaining in the adoption. Giving thanks to God. Recalling the Scripture of the 10 lepers who were cured and only one returned to Jesus to give thanks, I called our church secretary and asked if we could have a blessing in next Sunday's service. Of course, there was a resounding yes!

There is a brief time for announcements and special prayer requests or blessings after the sermon each Sunday. Father Jim motioned for us to come up when the path cleared out. We expected a simple prayer to give thanks and bless our official family. Barely noticeable in the back pews. Instead, we were presented with a small cross for each of the boys and a long-stemmed rose for Mom. Everyone stood up and clapped, sharing our joy. The boys seemed pretty confused over all the commotion but managed to stay reasonably composed for little boys. When it all died down, we went back to our pew and tried to return to normal worship.

I'm not sure how Father Jim managed to pull it together and resume the service. We could all hear the catch in his voice in the first few sentences. This had been a long journey for him too. Our church family had been with us in prayer support every step of the way. I wondered how people get through their struggles without that kind of TLC. This was definitely our church home.

The boys eventually became acolytes for the church services when they were old enough to follow directions and carry things in a procession. Of course, they were little angels when they were "on," but pew behavior on their Sundays off was another matter. Someone was always the subject of some type of harassment. I gave up on mediating and just learned to block and grab toys, pens, and other objects flying between them. JJ Watt would have been impressed.

A few years later, when they had finally passed that stage, I was attending a Holy Week service. Another Mom was going through the Wrestle Mania stage with her kids. Trying to ease her discomfort, I smiled and told her, "Don't worry about it. My kids were the same way at that age."

A gray-haired gentleman standing behind me couldn't resist commenting with a grin, "We remember!" Yup, definitely a church family. So glad I noticed that little church in our neighborhood so many years back.

Chapter Twenty-Six

HOMECOMING

I t was time for our trip to Arizona for the tribe's annual commemoration of their return to their native land. The boys didn't really understand what it was all about, but an excused time-out of school and the first time on a plane had them counting the days. We didn't know what to expect but were excited about the opportunity.

Getting three boys aged four to eight through the Houston airport was challenging, to say the least. They were much more interested in the gift shops and food court than getting to the gate to await boarding the plane. After buying enough candy for sufficient bribery and snatching more than one t-shirt by the collar, we were finally heading down the terminal.

The TSA officials looked at each other hoping we would get in someone else's lane. Screening these guys was going to take an expert. With lots of giggling, pushing, and throwing shoes in every direction, we made it through the line. I think they just gave up, figuring I couldn't possibly find time to be a terrorist. I was doing good to leave the house wearing shoes.

Their eyes were the size of silver dollars when they entered the plane. It's one thing to play with toy airplanes and wave at planes crossing over in the sky. Seeing how big it was from inside was mind blowing for them. Mark insisted on a window seat. He wasn't going to miss a single moment.

I had warned them about popping ears on takeoff and given them gum to chew. They seemed to handle it all okay and laughed at the weird feeling. Mark never took his eyes off the window the entire two-hour flight. He was fascinated, and his imagination was on overtime. Michael and Matthew were content to gobble down candy and sodas and play electronic games.

Arriving in Phoenix was the first half of the journey. I had reserved a soccer Mom minivan for the drive to the reservation. It's nestled in the mountains near Flagstaff, a straight shot up I-17. An easy drive with no highway changes, but uphill for the last 50 miles or so. I had never driven in mountains before and kept praying that our van was up to the challenge. If anything went wrong, we would be stranded in the middle of nowhere.

Of course, I had to give the boys the impression that everything was totally under control, and it was all tons of fun. Panic runs downhill and we were already battling gravity. They had never seen mountains before, and each curve brought more incredible scenery. The beauty made up for my Herculean grip on the steering wheel.

The tribe had a casino and motel along the highway. They had reserved a room for us, and I was anxious to get out of the van and get everyone settled in. Unfortunately, I went to the wrong entrance, and we all entered the casino. Security staff immediately encircled us and kept the boys from crossing the red line on the casino carpet, a huge no-no for anyone under 21. With total humiliation I explained we were looking for the motel lobby.

Somehow, they figured out that I wasn't a high roller. They politely escorted us to the motel lobby parking area so we could get checked in. Our friend, Theresa, from the tribal council was there to greet us. She escorted us to the front desk like we were royalty, and everything went very smoothly after that. Later I discovered that she held a very high position on the board of the casino. No wonder they all scurried to help us when she walked in!

She invited us to her home for dinner, a most welcome gesture. We would get to meet her family, which included the two little girls she had adopted. We followed her to the reservation entrance and on to her house. After being cooped up on the plane and in the car, the boys loved running around in the backyard showing off for the girls. They hung from tree branches like maniacs and tumbled everywhere.

After a wonderful dinner of burgers fixed on the charcoal grill, Theresa told me she had invited some of the boys' relatives to come over for an informal meeting. She hoped it would be all right. I reassured her that I was glad they would have the chance to get to know each other. Soon Yvette's brother and his family arrived. I stayed in the background with Theresa to give them time to be together. They were excited to meet their new family and connected easily. When they were leaving, they thanked us for the time together. Her brother also thanked me for taking in the boys and adopting them. He was so glad they were staying together and not separated in foster homes.

He explained what had happened with his siblings when they were young. They often went several months without seeing each other or knowing if everyone was okay. No wonder Yvette had made such a strong point in court that she wanted the boys to stay together, no matter what! We got back to the motel ready for some serious pillow time. It would be an early start in the morning. There was an annual ceremony that began at sunrise. I've never been a morning person but was totally committed to making the most of our three days. I wanted the boys to be immersed in the culture.

I should have read the brochure. So, about Day One. Everyone meets at the bottom of a very high cliff. At the top of the cliff is a natural spring that is very sacred to the tribe. The day begins with everyone able to climb heading up to reach it. Let's recap here. We're in the middle of the desert without any climbing gear. For that matter, no one else had any special gear either. It was freezing cold, as the desert tends to be in the morning. There were no handrails, ropes, or even a "Start Here" sign. It was just put a foot somewhere, grab something, or someone, and head up. Perfect for a city Mom with three little kids. And did I mention that I'm terrified of heights?

We could have waited politely at the base of the cliff with the elders. I knew better than to ask the boys. For them, this was better than Disney Land. They started shooting up the cliff before I could grab any of them. I slowly started up, terrified and wondering how I ever ended up in this situation. After making a little progress, I looked down hoping not to faint and said, "Be careful, boys. Stay close."

From countless feet above came the reply, "We're okay, Mom!" I finally made it up the cliff to join them at the spring. It did have a mystical sense about it. A freely flowing spring in the middle of the desert was definitely a gift from God. Everyone prayed silently at the spring. Then it was time to head back down to regroup with everyone for the rest of the ceremony. Did I mention there were no ropes?

No doubt I was the comic relief for the tribe that year. I grabbed everything and everyone possible on my descent. Again, the boys handled it like gazelles and thought Mom was hilarious. There was a spiritual ceremony afterward giving thanks for all of the year's blessings. The women formed one circle and the men formed another. At first, I kept the boys with me, being unsure what to do. Their uncle came over with a big smile and welcomed them to join the men's circle with him. They felt very grown up and part of the tribe.

By the time we returned to the motel it was lunch time. The cold had been replaced by desert heat. We got to thaw out. The boys wanted to get in the pool, but I hadn't packed any swim trunks. It was early March and I had thought it would be too cold to swim. I finally relented and let them jump in wearing their jeans. They thought that was awesome! I got approving nods and smiles from several tribal members. Maybe this crazy white lady from Houston was okay after all.

Midday the rest of the events started. It was two days of wonderful Native American dancers performing their cultural dances from tribes across the country. Traditional foods and crafts were everywhere, and the boys loved all of it. It turned out that their Great-Uncle, Vincent, who had met with us in Houston, was a revered elder of the tribe. He led the effort to retain their heritage with the younger generations. He was the emcee for the events, introducing the groups of dancers and explaining the significance of each type of dance that would be performed.

He spotted us sitting in the bleachers and made an announcement between dances. "We have very special visitors with us from Houston, Texas. Michelle Jenkins is here with her adopted boys,

Michael, Mark, and Matthew. They are Yvette's children. Please welcome them." Everyone clapped and cheered. His kind words made us feel like dignitaries instead of outsiders. We couldn't have been made any more welcome.

The final dance was for unity. Vincent called for everyone to come down from the bleachers and join in a huge circle to take hands and dance as one people. The boys had been dying to join in all day long and may have been the first ones to reach the dance area. It was very special to them, and the significance didn't escape them.

The next day they got an opportunity to have their picture taken with all of their male relatives. They were all seated next to the tribal seal. It was four generations, including a great-grandfather they had just met. They were thrilled to meet him and listen to his stories about his life. It was obviously a very special moment for him too.

It was time to get back in the minivan and pray that the brakes worked as well as the engine for our downhill journey back through the mountains. I had St. Christopher working overtime on that one. We made it back to the car rental return at the airport, and I wanted to kiss the concrete. I turned in the keys, looking at the debris left in the back seat. I had visions of a $200 cleaning charge, but they took pity on me.

The trip through the terminal returning home was much more sedated. The boys were exhausted from all the excitement. Mark even gave up the window seat. They went back to school the next week telling their friends and teachers all about their trip. It was clear that they had absorbed a lot of the culture and would retain the memories for the rest of their lives.

We would go back again, but nothing would ever compare with this initial experience. It had proven that cultures could meet and blend in wonderful harmony. God had brought us through an incredible journey to reach this point. We would always be thankful and give Him the praise and glory.

Chapter Twenty-Seven

THANK YOU FOR MICHAEL

T here's a weird thing about angels. They're mentioned over 200 times in the Bible. They're found in both the Old and New Testaments. It would be impossible to count the number of paintings depicting them, and their images are on countless bookmarks. Kids even make images of them in the snow, at least if they live above the Mason-Dixon line. So why does it sound so crazy to say someone in today's world has encountered an angel? Do people think they all retired? I'm not afraid to say that I truly believe I met one, and he was sent with a definite purpose. Hopefully you're not asking for a refund now on this book. Please bear with me.

We returned from our trip to Arizona and were trying to get into a normal routine. Of course, after Charlie's passing, we were trying to figure out what our new normal would be. I was doing my best to convince the boys that Mom had it all under control. That was a bold-faced lie, but they didn't need to know that. Michael had lived his first four years in total chaos with addicted parents and foster home shuffling. Then his next four years were finally in a reasonably calm home with us. So, the first half of his life had been crazy; the second half had been much better. Then Charlie passed and it had to take a big toll on his emerging sense of security. I knew it was hitting him hard, and I was doing everything I could to reassure him that he wasn't going to be going anywhere. We were still a family, and he was loved.

Mark had very little recollection of his earlier life. He was only two when he came to live with us. Matthew was three months old, so he had always known a normal family life. They both missed their Daddy a lot, but it didn't shake their world as badly as it did for Michael. For him it was sort of like the promo from the movie Jaws. "Just when you thought it was safe to go back in the water!" Naturally, he began acting out a lot, and it was taking every ounce of loving patience I could muster to help him.

Again, the march of the well-meaning folks ensued. I was frequently asked if I would be able to handle Michael on my own. Maybe I should consider placing him in institutional care and just raise Mark and Matthew. They assured me that it might be for the best for everyone. Even my pastor eventually suggested that I might need to sacrifice Michael to save the other two boys. Wow!

Remember those annoying KSBJ bumper stickers? Well, I've been listening to that Christian radio station for over 20 years now and still don't want to go through a day without it. While I was getting all of this *comforting* advice, a song from Phillips, Craig & Dean was popular. It was called "He Believes in Lost Causes" and every time it played it felt like God was talking directly to me through that radio.

I especially loved the line that "Common sense would just give up." That was pretty much where I was at the time. All the "common sense" folks were lining up with that advice. I was feeling outnumbered. The song helped me more than words can express, and I'm convinced an angel gave them those lyrics. They were definitely inspired.

So, back to *my* angel. It had been a long day and I was too tired to mess with dinner. The boys had way more energy than I did, so I did the only logical thing for a parent to do—go to McDonald's! The playground gave them a chance to run off steam while I could crash at the table. Dinner was instantly ready and there wasn't anything for them to complain about in their Happy Meals. Fortunately, they all got the same toy. We might just survive the evening.

While they were playing, a Hispanic man was sitting at a nearby table. He glanced over to me a few times with a warm smile. Now normally, that kind of attention from a stranger in a kid's play area would freak me out. Somehow, I felt totally at ease and smiled back. Then the move that would make any Mom yell "**Security!**" He walked over and pointed to the open chair at my table and asked in broken English if he could sit down. Yes, a sane person would have bolted, but for some reason I was completely okay with it.

Now I remember about 10 words from my high school Spanish. He had about the same size vocabulary in English. But, somehow, we managed to communicate with our pitiful verbal attempts and lots of hand gestures. He was clearly impressed with the boys and paid special attention to Michael. He asked their names. I still remembered "Como se llama." With each name he responded in Spanish, "Michael—Miguel; Mark—Marco; Matthew—Mateo."

As I've mentioned before, Michael had a Hispanic look to his features. Of course, he spoke English and didn't have any accent, so it was confusing to a lot of people who like to be able to peg everyone into a category. I had grown used to ignoring that and was trying to teach him to do the same. To us, he wasn't part Hispanic or part black or part anything. He was just Michael, he was part of our family, and he was loved.

Eventually my new companion got up to leave. Then he said something that will stick with me forever. It was as though he somehow knew our entire story. With a final big, warm smile he said, **"Thank you for Michael."** I was taken completely off guard. It was such a comforting thing to hear, but also quite a surprise. I glanced over to the boys in the playground. When I looked back, he was gone.

Now I don't mean he had left the table. I don't mean he had moved to the door. I don't mean he was walking away in the parking lot—he was gone!

My glance had only left him for a few seconds. I looked in every direction. Bear in mind that the play area was all windows, so I could see everywhere outside. Nothing. Now this was an average, 40-something looking guy. He certainly didn't look like a former Olympic track and field medalist. There's no way he could have taken off that quickly—unless he flew.

Wait a minute!

I didn't say anything to anyone about it for a long time. I figured the guys with the white coats would be giving me a special ride if I did. I just kept it to myself for a very long time, but pondered on it frequently.

I believed then, and always will, that he was an angel, sent to me with a simple, desperately needed message. It didn't matter anymore what other people thought. I could face a gauntlet of them. God had sent me a beautiful song and an angel. I got it!

A Final Thought to Share with You

I f you're struggling, waiting, or feeling all alone, I hope this book has helped you. It was written for YOU.

"I am writing to all who have been called by God the Father, who loves you and keeps you safe in the care of Jesus Christ" (**Jude 1:1b, NLT**).

Get out your magnifying glass if you need to and look for *your* breadcrumbs. I can promise you they are there.

"Do you not remember the five loaves for the five thousand, and how many baskets you gathered?" (Matthew 16:9b, ESV).

"And my God will meet all your needs according to the riches of his glory in Christ Jesus" (**Philippians 4:19, NIV**).

A song by TobyMac called "Help Is On The Way" sums it up. I, too, have lived enough life to say help is indeed on the way. This song has become my mantra. Yes, I do still have moments when I feel alone in my struggles. That's just part of being human. But looking back, I see all the times God rolled up his sleeves to work in my life and move mountains.

I remember He is always ready to do it again when I just have the sense and humility to ask for help. Then I start to see that fresh trail of breadcrumbs. I hope my story can give you that confidence for your life. When you can't see a way forward, look back. See all the times God has shone a light on your path and know He will continue. Follow your breadcrumbs!

Acknowledgments

This book is written to give thanks, glory, and praise to the Lord. We are eternally grateful for all of the people He sent to guide and help us through this journey. There is no way to mention everyone. These are a few of our breadcrumbs.

BRUCE D. PERRY, MD, PhD

https://www.bdperry.com/

Author, *What Happened To You?*, with Oprah Winfrey

You and your staff kept us stable throughout this journey. Your mediation with the members of the Tribal Council is beyond price, and we will always be grateful. Thank you for taking the time from your busy practice to write your very thoughtful foreword. You have been a blessing once again.

FULBRIGHT & JAWORSKI

https://www.nortonrosefulbright.com/en-us

We can never thank you enough for the tremendous efforts and heartfelt commitment of your team. Special thanks to Scott McKinney and Terriann Trostle.

JUSTICE FOR CHILDREN

https://justiceforchildren.org/

Your dedication to the best outcome for children at risk in the family courts is so vital. You made it possible for us to get the legal team we so desperately needed.

DAVID A. R. WHITE

http://davidarwhite.com/

Author, *God Is Not Dead*

Thank you for your three-point way to help identify God's purpose in our lives. You gave me the boost I needed to finish this book.

MICHAEL JR

https://michaeljr.com/

Author, *Life Is Funny*

Your talk at the Mission of Yahweh highlighting your many struggles on the way to success gave me the confidence to take on the work of writing this book. You were also very gracious in guiding me to your publisher so I could complete it.

MISSION OF YAHWEH

https://missionofyahweh.org/

Thank you for the incredible work that you do to change the lives of so many women and children. Your wonderful speakers at your annual fundraising luncheons, Michael JR, and David A. R. White, were definitely breadcrumbs for me to finish this task. *(If this book helped you, please donate to help continue their work.)*

SARAH WRONKO, MA

https://www.clearwindpublishing.com

Thank you for taking the time to talk to a totally unknown first-time author. Your interest and commitment have made this a success.

OUR COUNTLESS PRAYER WARRIORS

Thank you for carrying us through every step of our journey and continuing to do so even today. We wouldn't have made it without you.

KSBJ RADIO 89.3

Your ministry encouraged me every step of the way, and still does today. Thank you for your reminder that "God Listens."

About the Author

M ichelle Feagin has been a Houston resident since 1982 and a member of the Ascension Episcopal Church. She served on the Vestry and leads the Outreach committee and the Sunday prayer team. She also volunteers with their sponsored charities, including West Houston Area Ministries (WHAM), the Houston Food Pantry, and Mission of Yahweh.

Michelle has been blessed with three sons and four grandchildren. Most of her free time is spent enjoying her grandkids. She also enjoys jigsaw puzzles, cards, walking with her dogs, fishing, camping, and movies.

Michelle's key to success is focusing on listening to the questions and concerns of others. God gives us two ears and one mouth for a reason. She believes that faith and humor are the keys to working through any situation.

www.ingramcontent.com/pod-product-compliance
Lightning Source LLC
LaVergne TN
LVHW051020111025
823289LV00043B/707